ILLUSTRATED TALES OF
WALES

MARK REES

AMBERLEY

First published 2021

Amberley Publishing
The Hill, Stroud
Gloucestershire, GL5 4EP

www.amberley-books.com

British Library Cataloguing in Publication Data.
A catalogue record for this book is available from the British Library.

ISBN 978 1 4456 9722 2 (paperback)
ISBN 978 1 4456 9723 9 (ebook)

Typesetting by SJmagic DESIGN SERVICES, India.
Printed in Great Britain.

Contents

Introduction

A red and white dragon fighting tooth and claw in the night-time sky; a king so large he can walk across the ocean as easily as a stroll in the park; a charmed boy who transforms into a hare, an otter and a bird to outrun a wicked witch; and a kind-hearted mermaid who can save the lives of those in peril by calling their name three times.

These are the fantastical tales of Wales, the myths, legends and folk stories which have long fired the imagination of young and old alike. Yet while some of these yarns might be centuries old, they are in no way dusty old relics from the past. Storytelling is a living, breathing tradition which continues to evolve, and in this digital age it could be argued that the traditional Welsh tales are reaching a wider audience than ever.

For evidence of this, look no further than blockbuster book-to-screen adaptations like *Game of Thrones* and *The Witcher* where their influence can be keenly felt, or the many big-screen interpretations of the life of King Arthur and the Knights of the Round Table. Even the Welsh dragon itself is now a character in the Marvel superhero universe.

When I was in school, one of the most well-thumbed books in the library was a Welsh-language edition of the Mabinogion. This collection of medieval prose tales, which has inspired such heavyweights of the fantasy genre as J. R. R. Tolkien and C. S. Lewis, was fully illustrated with some wonderful art by Margaret Jones. But best of all – and I still can vividly remember first casting eyes upon it – was that the book was accompanied by a giant poster-size map of Wales which showed us exactly where each story took place.

Just imagine – not only were these incredible tales set here in Wales, right on our very doorstep, but thanks to this map we could now pinpoint the locations of the great battles, wild hunts and haunted caves, and explore them for ourselves.

It is this sense of wonder which comes from linking extraordinary stories with real-life places which has inspired my choice of tales in this book. I think it's one thing to say a man-eating serpent lurks in some top-secret waterfall, but it's something much more special when you can name that waterfall, take a photo of that waterfall, and provide directions to that waterfall so that the curious, or the foolhardy, can go on an adventure of their own.

This collection has been divided into five roughly equal-sized sections which, I hope, represent as wide a range of tales as possible from across the country, and have been gathered from many sources. Along with the Mabinogion these include Arthurian mythology and traditional folk and fairy tales, as well as some which have been passed on orally or recorded on public monuments, such as the memorial plaques in Beddgelert. As such, there are multiple variations of some of these stories, which throw up a few contradictions and alternative endings along the way, and where appropriate I have noted this throughout.

Once upon a time, Wales was an enchanted land of dragons, giants and sorcerers. By rediscovering these tales of old, or making new ones of our own, maybe we can look to re-enchant it once more.

Mark Rees, 2020

Legends of Wales

We begin our journey with a look at some of the more iconic people and places that can truly be considered legends of Wales. They are the larger-than-life monarchs who strolled across the ocean waves, the saints whose selfless actions saved the lives of humans and animals alike, and the bards who could transform shape at will to outsmart a vengeful enchantress. They are the mighty rulers, the valiant heroes, the snow-capped mountains and the fairy-tale castles at the heart of Welsh storytelling.

Taliesin, Chief of the Bards

The fine line between fact and fiction is often blurred in the old tales of Wales. This is no more evident than in the origin story of Taliesin, a legendary bard who travelled the land in the sixth century to regale the courts of kings with song and verse. Very much a real person, his words survive today in the fourteenth-century manuscript *Llyfr Taliesin (The Book of Taliesin)*, a collection of some of the earliest poems written in the Welsh language. Little is known about the man himself, however, although he is thought to have lived and died on the banks of Llyn Geirionydd on the edge of Gwydir Forest in Snowdonia National Park where a Taliesin Monument now stands.

The Taliesin Monument at Llyn Geirionydd. (Courtesy of ARG_Flickr under Creative Commons BY 2.0)

Llyn Tegid (Bala Lake). (Courtesy of Barry Skeates under Creative Commons BY 2.0)

It was in the sixteenth century that a fantastical account of his life first emerged and, if it is to be believed, might explain how he became such a wizard with words. The story begins on the banks of Llyn Tegid (Bala Lake) where Ceridwen, a powerful enchantress, lived with her husband Tegid Foel, who lends his name to the lake. They had two children: a daughter named Creirwy, who they considered to be exceedingly beautiful; and a son named Morfran, who they considered to be considerably less so. In fact, they thought he was frightfully ugly and, in the age of King Arthur and his chivalrous knights, saw this as a huge disadvantage in a world that placed great importance on physical attractiveness. As such, while they were sure that Creirwy would grow up to lead a very happy life, her brother would need a helping hand.

Ceridwen consulted her books of spells and decided that, while making him physically attractive was beyond her powers, she could compensate by giving him a brilliant brain instead. She found the instructions for an intricate potion which could bestow poetic inspiration, known as *Awen* in Welsh, on whoever drank the first three drops from it, and set about gathering the ingredients for her bubbling cauldron. The potion would need to boil for a year and a day precisely to be effective and, in order to complete the task, she would need the assistance of two volunteers. Her first helper was to be a hapless young boy named Gwion Bach,

Above left: A wooden carving of Taliesin by Simon O'Rourke at Pen y Bont Caravan and Camping in Bala. (Courtesy of Barry Skeates under Creative Commons BY 2.0)

Above right: A wooden carving of Ceridwen by Simon O'Rourke at Pen y Bont Caravan and Camping in Bala. (Courtesy of Barry Skeates under Creative Commons BY 2.0)

the son of Gwreang of Llanfair Caereinion, who was tasked with continuously stirring the potion. The second was a blind man named Morda, whose job was to keep the fire burning underneath the cauldron. Ceridwen herself would continue to gather the ingredients needed and add them to the brew daily.

The trio stuck to their tasks diligently for an entire year and, as the end drew near, Ceridwen grew increasingly excited. Her excitement soon turned to fury, however, when, with barely hours remaining, something totally unexpected happened. As Gwion stirred the cauldron on the eve of the final day, three drops of that magical potion – the very three drops needed to bring about poetical inspiration – splashed onto his hand. Ceridwen had kept the finer details of the spell a secret from her workers, and so Gwion had no idea what the consequences might be when he naturally put his hand to his mouth to suck up those three boiling droplets of liquid. The moment he did so, his life changed forever.

The potion worked like a charm, and Gwion's eyes were opened like never before. He could look into the past and foresee the future, and when he realised that he was in possession of a great power intended for another, his first action was to make a sharp exit. As he did so, the cauldron shattered in two and the remaining liquid turned to poison as it flowed away. When Ceridwen returned to discover her hard work undone, she lashed out at the innocent Morda, beating him so badly with a chunk of wood that one of the blind man's eyes dangled from its socket. She only relented when he was able to blurt forth what had really happened, and she stormed off in pursuit of Gwion.

By now the boy had discovered another of the advantages bestowed on him by the potion, the ability to transform into any creature at will, and took the form of a hare to nimbly run away. Not to be outdone, Ceridwen had exactly the same ability and transformed into a greyhound, for the start of what would prove to be a magical game of shape-shifting chase and catch. They eventually reached a river where, as they dived in, Gwion became a fish and Ceridwen became an otter. With his pursuer hot on his tail he leaped from the water and turned into a bird, while she swooped after him in the form of a hawk.

The increasingly desperate Gwion was given no rest and, when he noticed a heap of wheat down on the ground below, decided in what seemed like a moment of brilliance to change into a grain of wheat and disappear amongst the thousands of other similar seeds. The witch, however, had a cunning plan of her own, and Ceridwen became a high-crested black hen and scratched the ground until she found, and swallowed, the guilty seed. Quite unexpectedly, the seed began to grow inside her and, nine months later, she gave birth to a baby boy. On the one hand she despised the baby for all the trouble he had caused her and yet, when she looked down into its eyes, didn't have the heart to kill it.

She decided that the sea should decide his fate and on 29 April set him adrift in a leather bag to float along the River Dyfi towards the ocean. It was on the following day, the night before May Day, that Elffin ap Gwyddno was sent by his master Gwyddno Garanhir, Lord of Ceredigion, to catch salmon at the weir. He caught something much bigger instead: a child who he would raise as his own in Aberdyfi. He named him Taliesin, and he would grow to become known as the Chief of the Bards.

St Melangell, the Patron Saint of Hares

At the end of a winding valley deep in the Berwyn Mountains stands a church which contains the relics of Wales's patron saint of hares. Tucked away inside a shrine which has been described as the 'oldest Romanesque reliquary in northern Europe', this unique treasure can be found in St Melangell's Church, Pennant

Melangell, a Grade I listed place of worship which was founded in the eighth century near the village of Llangynog in Powys.

The twelfth-century shrine still exists today thanks to some quick-thinking from the local congregation who, during the Protestant Reformation when similar objects were being destroyed across Britain, dismantled it and hid it in the walls. The bones of the saint were buried in what is thought to be her original grave, and reinterred when it was safe to do so.

Another object of interest inside the church is an intricately designed fifteenth-century rood screen, which is illustrated with the legend of St Melangell herself. The events take place in the sixth century, when Brochwel Ysgithrog, the Prince of Powys, was out hunting with his hounds. As they rode through the forest they came across a young hare who, terrified for its life, fled as quickly as its legs would carry it. After leading its pursuers on a merry chase through the woods they came across a clearing in the trees, where a 'wondrous sight' caused them all to freeze in their tracks.

Kneeling on the ground was a beautiful maiden who was so deeply absorbed in her prayers that she failed to notice the arrival of her visitors. She was dressed in a long flowing garment which swept out on the ground all around her, and the hare leaped into its folds to hide from the dogs. But it did more than simply

St Melangell's Church. (Courtesy of the National Churches Trust under Creative Commons BY 2.0)

Above: Pennant Melangell. (Courtesy of Edward Crompton under Creative Commons BY-SA 2.0)

Below: A hare out for a run in the Severn Valley. (Courtesy of Kumweni under Creative Commons BY 2.0)

protect the creature, and filled it with a sense of bravery which caused it to turn and stare defiantly at its pursuers. The prince urged his dogs onwards, but they did the exact opposite. The hounds, which moments before had been snarling and snapping at the heels of their prey, meekly backed away and fled with a whimper. He attempted to blow his horn, but it stuck to his lips and no sound was forthcoming.

Amazed at the turn of events, the prince approached the woman and demanded to know who she was, and what she was doing on his land. In a softly spoken voice she replied that her name was Melangell, the daughter of a king of Ireland. Her father had arranged for her to marry one of his men, but having sworn to a life of celibacy in the name of God she instead fled across the waves in search of solitude. With the Lord watching over her, she was guided safely to this very spot where she had been living a peaceful life of piety without seeing the face of another person for fifteen years.

The prince, who could feel a heavenly power emanating from her, was deeply touched by Melangell's story. Convinced that it must have been divine intervention that saved the hare from his ravening hounds he gifted her his lands in which to establish a safe haven for all those in need, both humans and animals alike. She remained there for the rest of her life where she lived as a hermit and slept on a bare rock at night. Her body was later laid to rest at the nearby church.

Melangell is credited with performing many a miracle on behalf of those who sought comfort in the Kingdom of Powys, and was venerated as a saint in 590. Her feast day is on 27 May, and as the patron saint of hares she is seen as the protector of these animals, who themselves became known as Oen Melangell, which is Welsh for Melangell's lambs.

Branwen, Daughter of Llŷr

The name Branwen has long been a popular choice for a baby girl in Wales. Yet what those who are lucky enough to be called Branwen might not realise is that their name is thought to mean fair or beautiful raven, and that they share it with a legendary hero who played a major role in the medieval tales of the Mabinogion.

The story of Branwen, Daughter of Llŷr (Branwen, ferch Llŷr), begins on the shores of Harlech, where her big brother – quite literally her big brother, he's a giant – Brân the Blessed (Bendigeidfran), stares thoughtfully out to sea. The monarch is watching a fleet of thirteen ships approach his land, one of which is carrying Matholwch, the king of Ireland, who upon being welcomed ashore asks Brân for his sister's hand in marriage. A council is hastily convened in nearby Aberffraw to discuss the union and it is agreed that, as the marriage will unite the two warring countries, the offer should be accepted.

A lavish party is thrown to mark the occasion, but things turn sour very quickly when Efnysien, Brân and Branwen's half-brother, arrives home to discover that the decision was made without him being consulted. In a fit of rage he takes his revenge by savagely maiming the horses of the Irish visitors with a knife, and

Harlech Beach. (Courtesy of Ed Webster under Creative Commons BY 2.0)

an outraged Matholwch immediately calls off the wedding and prepares to sail home. Brân is only able to pacify his Irish counterpart with a series of increasingly extravagant gifts, the most impressive of which is the famed Pair Dadeni (the Cauldron of Rebirth), a miraculous cauldron with the power to revive the dead. There was just one catch, of which Matholwch was unaware: anyone brought back to life by the cauldron would be deaf and mute afterwards.

With calm restored the pair were soon wed, and Matholwch returned to the Emerald Isle with his bride in tow. Life was good for Branwen to begin with, who was treated with kindness and gave birth to a baby boy named Gwern. All was not so well with her husband, however, who could not shake off the niggling feeling that Efnysien had made him a laughing stock when he wounded his horses, and he believed that people were snickering at him behind his back. He vented his anger on his wife by stripping her of her royal comforts and banishing her to work in the kitchens like a slave, and adding insult to injury, he even ordered the butcher to slap her on the ear once a day with his bloodstained hands after cutting the meat. Her only source of comfort came in the form of a kind starling who visited her in her captivity. She tamed and trained the bird to deliver messages, and sent it across the Irish Sea to tell her brother of her plight. It found Brân in Caernarfon, where the remains of Segontium Roman Fort now stand, and upon hearing the sorrowful message he swiftly gathered an army and set off to her rescue.

Brân was gigantic in size even for a giant and had no need of a boat to cross the water, simply wading through the sea with his ships following behind. Matholwch was in no mood for a fight and, when word reached him that the head of a giant had been seen making its way towards the land, he made a hasty retreat. In order to thwart his pursuers he destroyed a bridge behind him, but it would take more

Harlech Castle. (Courtesy of Mike Cartmell under Creative Commons BY 2.0)

than that to stop the encroaching army. In one of the more iconic moments of the Mabinogion, Brân responds by lying down and using his own body as a bridge on which his army can cross.

When they eventually caught up with Matholwch he tried to broker a deal. Not only would he treat Branwen with the respect she deserved, but he would relinquish the crown of Ireland and pass it on to their son, thus ensuring a new dawn for the warring nations. Branwen only wanted the best for her boy and pleaded with her brother to agree to the offer, to which he eventually did. Peace, it appeared, was within touching distance, but there was to be one final sting in the tail.

As a sign of their renewed friendship Matholwch had a super-sized home built for his brother-in-law which would accommodate his giant frame. But while the rulers might have agreed to a truce, there were still many Irish elders unhappy with the situation and conceived of a plan to kill Brân by hiding in his new abode and attacking him when he least expected it. It might have worked as well had it not been for the loose cannon Efnysien, who visited first in order to inspect the property. When he found them hiding inside sacks disguised as flour he crushed their heads one by one, and followed it up with his most catastrophic and brutal act of all. During a feast in honour of the newly appointed king he suddenly grabbed his nephew by the feet and threw him to the flames of the open fire. Branwen could only watch on in despair as her son burned to death.

An almighty fight broke out in which the Irish were slaughtered, but they had a secret weapon up their sleeves: the Pair Dadeni, which could be used to revive the dead soldiers as deaf and mute zombies. This turned the tide in their favour, and as his comrades fell all around him, Efnysien finally realised that he might

Aberffraw. (Courtesy of Phil Brown under Creative Commons BY 2.0)

have been the cause of all this unnecessary suffering. He vowed to put things right once and for all and disguised himself as one of the dead Irish fighters in order to have his own body flung into the magical cauldron. As he was thrown in, he sprang to life and grabbed hold of the edges, using the last of his energy to push with all his might and shatter it into four quarters. Not only did he put an end to its powers of reincarnation, but to his own life at the same time. His sacrifice spurred on those still fighting to victory and, with the battle won, the few remaining survivors – Brân, Branwen and seven brave men – began the journey home.

It was during the voyage back to the Island of the Mighty that Brân realised he had been mortally wounded during the fight by a poisoned dart. He would soon be dead and asked for his head to be buried at Bryn Gwyn in London, where the Tower of London is now thought to stand, and turned to face France in order to ward off invasion. Branwen, meanwhile, having lost her brother, half-brother and son in one fell swoop, died of a broken heart on that same fateful journey home during a stop on Anglesey. A ring cairn in Llanddeusant called Bedd Branwen (Branwen's Grave) is said to be her final resting place.

A statue of Brân carrying the body of his nephew Gwern can be seen outside Harlech Castle, sculpted by Ivor Roberts-Jones in 1984.

Above: The remains of Segontium Roman Fort in Caernarfon. (Courtesy of Anne-Lise Heinrichs under Creative Commons BY 2.0)

Below: The Mabinogion statue outside Harlech Castle. (Courtesy of Andrew Bowden under Creative Commons BY 2.0)

A Night on Cadair Idris

Cadair Idris is a majestic mountain with a deadly secret. Looming large in the south of Snowdonia National Park, by the light of day it is a place of awe-inspiring natural beauty, but after the shades of night have fallen it becomes far less welcoming. For legend tells us that, if anyone is foolish enough to spend the night alone on its summit, they could lose their mind, or even their life, by the time the cock crows the next morning.

Standing at 893 metres high, Cadair Idris is the second highest mountain in Wales. Towering over the Gwynedd town of Dolgellau, its name translates as the Chair of Idris, and the Idris in question is thought to be Idris ap Gwyddno, a real-life seventh-century prince who was also known by the more menacing nickname Idris Gawr, which means Idris the Giant. According to folklore, he was so gigantic that the chair on which he sat was formed by three peaks of the mountain, namely the summit of Penygader, which means the head of the chair; Mynydd Moel, the bare mountain; and Cyfrwy, the saddle which overlooks Llyn y Gadair, a shallow lake famed for being a hotspot for Welsh fairy folk the *Tylwyth Teg*. At the foot of the mountain were three enormous stones called Tre Greienyn, which had been grains of rock shaken from the giant's shoe, while his final resting place, Gwely Idris (Idris' Bed), is hidden away nearby.

Idris himself was a poet and an astronomer, and would observe the heavens from his observatory high on the mountain. Gazing at the cosmos from such a lofty position was a profound experience that inspired his verses, but so intense are the feelings of awe that it inspires in its viewers that if a lesser person were to attempt to do the same it could prove deadly.

Cadair Idris's Cyfrwy peak and Llyn y Gadair lake. (Courtesy of ARG_Flickr under Creative Commons BY 2.0)

Cadair Idris's eastern edges from below. (Courtesy of ARG_Flickr under Creative Commons BY 2.0)

View from Crib Goch of the stepped plateau summit of Cadair Idris above the Mawddach Estuary. (Courtesy of ARG_Flickr under Creative Commons BY 2.0)

According to tradition, if anyone other than Idris sleeps on the mountain's summit then one of three things will happen. The first, and the best-case scenario, is that they would wake up as a poet or a genius, with a new-found mastery of the word and the world. The second, and a far less desirable scenario, is that they would wake up raving mad, and spend the rest of their days out of their minds. Finally, and by far the worst-case scenario, was that they would not wake up at all – there was a one-in-three chance that they would be rewarded with nothing but death.

Llyn Gwernan. (Courtesy of Tanya Dedyukhina under Creative Commons BY 3.0)

On one occasion, a group of farmers from Llanegryn were making their way home from Dolgellau fair when they saw a 'remarkable sight' at Llyn Gwernan, a lake at the foot of Cadair Idris. Circling the water was a 'great man, with green water weeds entwined in his hair, and naked save for a girdle of green weeds'. As he walked he repeated to himself 'The hour is come but the man is not, the hour is come but the man is not.' This was a little bit too strange for the farmers, who upped their pace and sped off home, and the next day they discovered that others had also seen the strange man who continued to pace and complain all night until 5 a.m.

A few days later, much darker news from the lake reached the village. The dead body of a man had been found floating in the water, and it was someone that the locals recognised. Earlier that week an outsider had arrived in town asking about the prophesy attached to the mountain and, despite being warned against it, set off to spend the night there alone. He was not seen alive again. What exactly happened is unknown, but it is assumed that the experience drove him mad and that, while in a delirious state, he encountered the mumbling man dressed in weeds who dragged him down to his watery grave.

There are some who say that rather than going mad on the mountain he must have been mad to begin with, as no sane man would have attempted such a feat in the first place.

In Search of Hidden Treasure

For those who know where to look, there is hidden treasure that could make you rich beyond your wildest dreams to be found all across Wales. From the deepest lakes to the highest mountains, there are jewels, swords, and all manner of valuables just waiting to be discovered.

But before you set off in search of these riches, be warned: such wealth is rarely claimed easily and, more often than not, is guarded by such forces that only the foolhardy would dare to mess with.

Take, for example, the tale of untold wealth buried beneath the fairy-tale castle of Castell Coch on the outskirts of Cardiff. The fortress as we see it today dates from the nineteenth century, but the Gothic Revival towers were built on the foundations of a much older castle which, so legend tells us, was created for Ifor Bach, the Lord of Senghenydd, back in the twelfth century.

He ruled there from the day it was completed until his final breath, but was deeply concerned about who would look after his body, as well as his many belongings, after he'd shuffled off this mortal coil. He became so morbidly obsessed with the idea that thieves would steal all he had amassed that he took the extreme measure of transforming two of his guards into stone eagles to watch over him in the afterlife. When the fateful day arrived, he was laid to rest deep below the castle with his treasure for company and his two guardian eagles for protection. His suspicions proved to be well founded, and when two foolish burglars attempted to break into his tomb they paid dearly when the stone beasts magically sprang to life and ensured they wouldn't be stealing anything from anyone ever again.

Another story of buried treasure took place in the mountains of Snowdonia, where a shepherd came across a dark and mysterious cave near Llyn Ogwen. Despite knowing better than to enter such strange places alone, curiosity got the better of him and he creeped inside where, to his amazement, he found a seemingly endless supply of vessels made from the finest bronze. He quickly tried to fill his arms with as many as he could carry, but there was just one snag: as he reached out to pick up the first one, he discovered that it was too heavy for him to move. So heavy that even with all his strength he was unable to budge even a single item, and was forced to leave empty-handed. He resolved to return with some strong friends the next day and, upon leaving, concealed the entrance with stones and left a trail of wood chips with which to retrace his steps. When he returned, however, the wood chips had all been removed by the magical creatures who were guarding the treasure for its rightful owner, and he never found the entrance again.

Elsewhere in Snowdonia, a secret cave was also discovered near Marchlyn Mawr by a farmer from Rhiwen in Gwynedd. According to local lore the treasure of King Arthur is stashed somewhere near the lake behind Elidir Fawr mountain, and when he peered inside and saw a great mound of untold riches he couldn't believe his luck. He rushed in eagerly with outstretched arms to claim the loot for himself, but as he did so a deafening clap of thunder filled the air and an unnatural darkness descended.

Castell Coch. (Courtesy of Haydn Blackey under Creative Commons BY 2.0)

Right: Castell Coch through the trees. (Courtesy of Jam Roly-Poly under Creative Commons BY-ND 2.0)

Below: Llyn Ogwen. (Courtesy of William Hook under Creative Commons BY-SA 2.0)

Marchlyn Mawr from Elidir Fawr. (Courtesy of Nathan Jones under Creative Commons BY-SA 2.0)

He was left to blindly fumble around for the entrance, and once outside found that a terrifying storm had cast a black shadow across the land. It was violently whipping up the waves on the lake and, as he watched the choppy waters crash all around, saw what appeared to be a coracle sailing towards him. As he looked closer he noticed that it carried three of the most beautiful women he had ever seen standing upon it, but they were not alone. Equal to their beauty was the ugliness of the man who crouched before them, and appeared to be guiding the boat towards the mouth of the cave and the farmer himself.

The sight of this grotesque creature was enough to cause him to flee in terror empty-handed and, while he did manage to escape safely, he was never the same again. His health suffered terribly, and just the mere mention of the lake's name was enough to send him into a fit of panic.

Fantastic Beasts

If the legends are to be believed, Wales was once populated by a veritable bestiary of weird and wonderful animals. Much like the human heroes which protected the land, these beasts could also be both valiant and brave, with one heroic dog truly living up to the moniker of 'man's best friend'. At the same time, there were also curious creatures who were much more wicked in nature, and were best avoided at all costs. Then there were those who fall somewhere in between, like the horse-skulled Mari Lwyd which continues to haunt the streets today.

The Dragons of Dinas Emrys

Have you ever wondered why there's a red dragon on the national flag of Wales?

Y Ddraig Goch, to give it its Welsh name, has long been synonymous with the country, and some say that the fire-breathing serpent was the symbol of choice of the legendary hero King Arthur. From a more historical perspective, its origins could be traced back as far as the Roman occupation when the military used a dragon on their standard, while Owain Glyndŵr, the last native Welshman to hold the title of Prince of Wales, proudly displayed a golden dragon on his banner.

Welsh flags for St David's Day. (Courtesy of the National Assembly for Wales under Creative Commons BY 2.0)

The earliest known story to feature the red dragon protecting its homeland is Lludd and Llefelys, one of the medieval prose tales collected in the Mabinogion. It starts in Caer Lludd, or London as the English capital is better known today, where Lludd, the king of Britain, is being troubled by three plagues which are devastating his lands. He turns to his wiser brother Llefelys, the ruler of Brittany, for advice, who explains that one of the plagues, a terrible shriek which fills the air every May Day, is being caused by two dragons fighting in the skies above – the country's native red dragon, and a foreign white dragon which has invaded its territory. As a result, the blood-chilling noise they created as they battled was striking fear into the hearts of men, leaving the women childless, and driving the young folk out of their minds, while the animals died, the plants withered, and the water dried up.

In order to rid his land of these creatures he was instructed to find the country's halfway point, which proved to be the city of Oxford, and to build a giant ditch there in which to conceal a huge cauldron of mead. This is where the dragons would fight overhead and, when they became exhausted, would swoop down and drink their fill, eventually falling asleep. A satin cover could then be tied around the quarrelsome reptiles who could be safely buried deep out of harm's way.

The plan worked perfectly; Lludd buried the dragons deep in the heart of the Snowdonian mountains, and they all lived happily ever after. Well, for a short while at least, anyway. The story is picked up again in *The History of the Britons*, which is

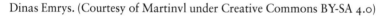

Dinas Emrys. (Courtesy of Martinvl under Creative Commons BY-SA 4.0)

thought to have been written early in the ninth century, by which time the country is being ruled by the tyrant Vortigern. Having assisted the Saxons in their invasion of Wales, the less-than-popular monarch is forced to flee for his own safety, and finds the perfect spot in which to settle in the mountains of Snowdonia.

He sets his men to work on building a lavish fortress on a wooded hillock just outside the village of Beddgelert but, despite slaving away all day, whenever they arrive for work again the next morning their efforts from the previous day have been destroyed, forcing them to begin anew. Vortigern grew weary with the delay, and when he turned to his royal magicians for advice their response was very dire indeed. He was told that his betrayal of his people had displeased the gods, and the only way to appease them was with a human sacrifice. More specifically, he would need to spill the blood of a boy who was born without a father on the site of the building or it would never remain standing.

A suitable child named Emrys Wledig was found, but this boy was wiser than his years suggested and, before he was killed, convinced the ruler that his advisors were wrong. It wasn't the displeased gods who were causing the trouble but two dragons who were fighting underneath the hillock – the very same dragons

The ruins of an eleventh-century tower on Dinas Emrys. (Courtesy of Aetheling1125 under Creative Commons BY-SA 3.0)

The gorge at Dinas Emrys. (Courtesy of Aetheling1125 under Creative Commons BY-SA 3.0)

which Lludd had buried there. It sounded like an unlikely story, but Vortigern was determined to put an end to the matter once and for all and went in search of these dragons. Not only did he find them but he released them from their underground prison, and they immediately soared upwards to resume their battle as if no time had passed.

Emrys explained that their fighting was a prophesy in which the red dragon, who symbolised the native Britons, would eventually rout the white dragon, who represented the invading Saxons. In some versions of the tale he then reveals his true identity to be none other than Myrddin Emrys, more commonly known as Merlin the wizard, and the hillock on which they stood became known as Dinas Emrys. The victorious red dragon, meanwhile, became the national symbol of Wales.

The Water Horse of Wales

If you look closely at the ocean waves during stormy weather you might, just might, catch a glimpse of one of Wales's more mysterious supernatural creatures. As the waves crash against the rocks the Ceffyl Dŵr, or Water Horse of Wales, gallop along in the sea's foam, and the wild conditions are reflected in the colour of their coats which range from the snow-white of the spray to the dapple-grey of the thunder clouds.

These four-legged entities are said to haunt some of Wales's more idyllic waterside locations, and at first glance they might appear to be harmless enough. Appearances, however, can be deceiving, and that's certainly the case when it comes to these small horses, and the only real tell-tale sign that gives them away is their hooves which, like the Devil's, point the wrong way.

When encountered, the best plan of action is to leave them in peace and be on your way. The worst plan of action is to attempt to mount them, as they have been known to severely punish those who take the liberty of riding on their backs. They do this by charging at breakneck speed across the land, or by literally taking flight and soaring high into the sky before suddenly evaporating into thin air, leaving their passenger to plummet to a rather gruesome end.

In the nineteenth century, one weary traveller was making his way through Glynneath when he decided to rest his tired bones near a waterfall in an area known as Waterfall Country. As he made himself comfy he noticed what appeared

Stormy seas at Porthcawl. (Courtesy of Jeremy Segrott under Creative Commons BY 2.0)

to be the apparition of a horse emerging from behind the cascading water, which glistened in the sunshine as it shook the spray from its mane. It was such a fine specimen that something deep inside compelled him to approach and mount it and, as soon as he had done so, the horse sprang into action and sped off at an unbelievably fast speed.

The man, who was holding on for dear life, found the experience to be quite exciting to begin with. But as his ride showed no signs of slowing down or tiring – if anything it was doing the opposite and running faster and faster – his exhilaration soon turned to apprehension and, as they flashed along at the speed of lightning, to terror. So swiftly was the creature moving that its hooves no longer appeared to touch the ground, and onwards it ran until the sun in the sky had been replaced by the moon.

Just as he felt he could take no more the horse came to an abrupt halt and flung its traveller onto a nearby hill. He looked back in disbelief as his ride became ever-more indistinct and faded into nothing but a faint vapour. The disorientated man walked for a mile to the nearest village, where he discovered that he was now in Llanddewi Brefi. In the space of an hour he had been carried to Ceredigion, a journey which would take almost twice as long nowadays in a car on modern roads.

A similar incident took place many centuries before on the site of a Roman camp near Brecon. It was on the banks of the River Honddu where an unsuspecting man was enticed onto the back of a small grey horse and, before

Pontneddfechan, Glynneath. (Courtesy of Richard Jones under Creative Commons BY-SA 2.0)

Above: River Honddu. (Courtesy of Claire Cox under Creative Commons BY-ND 2.0)

Below: River Tywi. (Courtesy of Leon Wilson under Creative Commons BY 2.0)

he knew it, was being whizzed across the country only to be thrown off on the banks of the River Tywi just outside Carmarthen. Unable to retrace his steps he was forced to wait for three days until the horse reappeared to carry him back, but the return journey was far from an easy ride. The man found himself dragged through the water, brambles and foliage, to such an extent that he was barely recognisable by the end of the ordeal.

The banks of the River Tywi were said to be something of a favoured haunt for the Ceffyl Dŵr, and in another account a man who went to work in a coracle returned home that night riding a horse 'which had eyes like balls of fire, and a snort like a blast'. This more frightening variation of the creature was more common in the northern half of the country, where some considered it to be a 'terror of the night'. It even had the ability to shape-shift into other animals such as a goat, a squirrel, or a frog, or even a combination of creatures, such as in one particularly creepy tale where an 'indescribable' man-goat figure nearly crushed people to death.

If that wasn't scary enough, in the old county of Caernarfonshire they were said to 'fraternise' with the local mountain ponies, and that the small horses which can be seen roaming in the area today are direct descendants of the Ceffyl Dŵr.

Gelert, the Faithful Hound

The tale of Gelert, the faithful hound who paid the ultimate price for his life-saving heroics, is one of Wales's best-known, and heartbreakingly tragic, legends. It tells of how man's best friend fought a fierce and bloody fight to the death with a giant wolf to protect the baby son of his master Prince Llywelyn the Great, but who mistakenly assumed that Gelert had killed his child and lashed out in grief, piercing the wolfhound with his sword.

The setting for the tragedy is Beddgelert, a picturesque village in Gwynedd which also shares its name with the valiant dog. The word *bedd* means grave in Welsh and, combined with the name Gelert, translates as Gelert's Grave. A monument to the dog can be found beneath a tree at the popular tourist hotspot, where the following account is inscribed in both Welsh and English on tablets placed on the grave:

> In the 13th century Llewelyn, prince of North Wales, had a palace at Beddgelert. One day he went hunting without Gelert, 'The Faithful Hound', who was unaccountably absent.
>
> On Llewelyn's return the truant, stained and smeared with blood, joyfully sprang to meet his master. The prince alarmed hastened to find his son, and saw the infant's cot empty, the bedclothes and floor covered with blood.
>
> The frantic father plunged his sword into the hound's side, thinking it had killed his heir. The dog's dying yell was answered by a child's cry.
>
> Llewelyn searched and discovered his boy unharmed, but nearby lay the body of a mighty wolf which Gelert had slain. The prince filled with remorse is said never to have smiled again. He buried Gelert here.

Above: People gather at Gelert's Grave in Beddgelert. (Courtesy of Keith Ruffles under Creative Commons BY 3.0)

Right: Gelert's Grave beneath the trees in Beddgelert. (Courtesy of Peta Chow under Creative Commons BY 2.0)

Above left: Detail of Gelert's Grave in Beddgelert. (Courtesy of Peta Chow under Creative Commons BY 2.0)

Above right: Gelert's Statue, near Gelert's Grave in Beddgelert. (Courtesy of Ken Bagnall under Creative Commons BY-SA 2.0)

It's enough to bring a tear to the eye of even the most hard-hearted of visitors, but there is some good news for animal lovers – the story is almost certainly not true, and Gelert is probably not buried under that tree, or anywhere else for that matter. In fact, the story is not entirely unique to Wales, and variations of these 'faithful hound' tales can be found across Europe, where the setting and names change, but the events remain practically the same.

The Welsh spin on the story is thought to have been conceived late in the eighteenth century by the landlord of a local pub, whose aim was nothing more than to drum up a little extra tourism for the area. David Pritchard, the proprietor of the Royal Goat Inn, claimed that Gelert was buried under a burial cairn, and hastily erected one. It did the trick, and not only did he presumably sell a few extra pints, but it continues to draw sightseers to Snowdonia National Park today. As for the name Beddgelert, doubt has also been cast on the dog's role in that as well, and it is considered more likely that it relates to a local seventh-century Celtic saint.

Regardless of its authenticity, it remains one of Wales's more enduring and popular legends, and is a constant source of inspiration for the visitors who travel from far and wide to the village as a result. In the nineteenth century the English poet William Robert Spencer composed a ballad in Gelert's honour, which was also set to music by the celebrated composer Joseph Haydn, and the final verse correctly predicted that Gelert would live long in the memory:

> And, till great Snowdon's rocks grow old,
> And cease the storm to brave,
> The consecrated spot shall hold
> The name of 'Gêlert's Grave.'

The Winged Beast of the Waterfall

In times gone by, dragons weren't the only winged reptiles terrorising the skies of Wales.

All manner of snake-like beasts were seen weaving their way through the heavens above, and for many people the most terrifying of them all was known as a gwiber or gwybr. These silent assassins would float among the clouds until they were ready to swoop, and the only warning sign their victims received was the sudden appearance of their gigantic shadow on the ground below. When the time was just right they'd dive down from their lofty position and devour their targets, which could include as many as an entire flock of sheep or a herd of cattle in one fell swoop.

In 1887, the Revd Elias Owen wrote that these deadly creatures had once been common snakes but 'having drunk the milk of a woman, and by having eaten of bread consecrated for the Holy Communion, became transformed into winged serpents'. They were said to prefer living near the water, and while their colour could vary were often a shade of silvery white which helped camouflage them in their watery domains.

One such creature was plaguing the village of Llanrhaeadr-ym-Mochnant in the northern tip of Powys. It lived in an idyllic spot near Llyn Lluncaws lake above Pistyll Rhaeadr Waterfalls, an 80-metre high waterfall and one of the 'Seven Wonders of Wales', yet dwelling in this place of beauty did nothing to soothe its temper. This was a particularly nasty form of gwiber which, far from being content with pursuing farm animals for prey, had begun to turn its attentions towards the villagers themselves.

Its reign of terror had to be brought to an end, and so the locals got together to think of a solution. As each plan failed they grew increasingly desperate, and left the village to seek the advice of a wise woman who lived in the nearby hills. She explained that the colour red could be used to lure such creatures into a trap, in much the same way as a red rag could be used to anger a bull, and her plan was to attach giant spiked collars to a large standing stone and then conceal them with a big red cloth. A circle of fire should then be lit around it, which would not only make the trap even easier for the gwiber to spot from

Opposite: Pistyll Rhaeadr waterfall. (Courtesy of ARG_ Flickr under Creative Commons BY 2.0)

Above: The base of Pistyll Rhaeadr waterfall. (Courtesy of Antonio Vianello under Creative Commons BY 2.0)

Right: The water at Pistyll Rhaeadr waterfall. (Courtesy of Peter Black under Creative Commons BY-SA 2.0)

the sky, but give the illusion of a fire-breathing dragon trespassing on its patch, thus provoking a violent reaction from their adversary who would attack the stone and skewer themselves on the hidden spikes.

They all agreed that it was the best idea so far and set to work. The men created the giant spiked collars while the women sewed the enormous red covering, and after both were wrapped around the pillar a fire was lit. The plan worked perfectly and the infuriated monster swooped down and began to strike its enemy with increasingly frenzied blows, while its unmovable opponent simply stood there. After hours of one-sided fighting the gwiber collapsed on the ground from exhaustion and loss of blood, and peace was restored to the land. The standing stone became known as Pillar Coch – the red pillar.

A view from the top of Pistyll Rhaeadr waterfall. (Courtesy of David Harris under Creative Commons BY 2.0)

The Secrets of the Mari Lwyd

Christmas is a time for family, friends, and goodwill to all. In Wales, it is also a time for one of the world's more unusual-looking folk traditions to emerge, when the creature dubbed the 'Welsh ghost horse' is let loose to playfully terrorise the local community.

The Mari Lwyd is a wassailing custom which involves attaching a decorated horse's skull to a pole and parading it door to door to challenge the neighbours to a battle of musical rhymes. Traditionally it takes to the streets on New Year's Eve or the days leading up to Twelfth Night to mark the end of the year, although in recent times it has come to be associated with the Christmas season in general, and is making increasingly regular appearances at Welsh cultural events throughout the year, such as at Nos Calan Gaeaf (Halloween).

Its name, which is sometimes spelt Mari Llwyd and Mary Lwyd, is thought to mean either Grey Mare or Blessed Mary, both of which would make the creature feminine, and with the latter suggesting a Christian influence. While its origins are shrouded in mystery, Marie Trevelyan does write that 'in the far past' a woman impersonating the Virgin Mary was present at the procession, as was Joseph and the baby Jesus. She also notes that as far back as the seventeenth century it was known as the 'Marw Llwyd', which translates as the much more menacing-sounding Grey Death, and could have its roots in ancient Celtic beliefs about the dying of the year.

The earliest known records of the custom date from the start of the nineteenth century, when groups of men and boys would decorate their horse skulls, ideally

A trio of Mari Lwyds waiting to cause some mischief. (Courtesy of SWWMedia)

The Mari Lwyd is led through the orchard at the Gower Heritage Centre. (Courtesy of Liz Barry)

Wassailing at the Gower Heritage Centre. (Courtesy of Liz Barry)

a real skull but, if one could not be found, straw and rags could be used, with ribbons, rosettes, bells and glass for eyes. Once completed a member of the gang would take on the role of the Mari herself, which involved holding the skull aloft like a hobby horse while concealed under a white sheet, and another would take on the part of the leader. In stark contrast to the Mari they would be finely dressed in a hat and suit, much like a bridegroom, and would carry a whip or similar implement with which to control the lively mare. The remaining members would deck themselves out in face paint and colourful adornments, with some carrying instruments to be played along the way, all of which has been compared to a Punch and Judy (or Siwan as she is also known in Wales) performance.

Under the cover of darkness they would knock on doors and try to gain access to houses by singing a Welsh-language song known as *pwngco*. A rhyming battle of wits, the visitors would sing a verse, known as an *awen*, in which they demanded to be let in, while the occupiers would attempt to repel them with a *verse* of their own.

The Mari Lwyd after dark at the Chepstow Wassail and Mari Lwyd. (Courtesy of Andy Dingley under Creative Commons BY-SA 3.0)

These verses would typically be witty and sarcastic ditties of how hard life had been, with the visitors bemoaning that they had no cake and beer for Christmas and were in need of some festive charity, while those inside insisted that they had been through a rough patch themselves and had barely enough to sustain their household. If successful in gaining entry the gang would be rewarded with food and drink while the Mari caused a bit of high-spirited mayhem, and with their thirst and hunger temporarily sated they would sing a parting song of thanks and be on their way.

Those wishing to experience the Mari Lwyd in action nowadays, albeit in a slightly more respectable manner, can visit one of the many places where the tradition has been revived. One of the longest running is the Old House Inn in the village of Llangynwyd near Maesteg, who welcome the Mari Lwyd on New Year's Eve. A wassailing festival at Gower Heritage Centre in Parkmill, Gower, sees many horse-skulled visitors descend on the peninsula each January, where tradition tells us that the horse's skull should be buried in the ground afterwards in order to be dug up and reused the following year. Possibly the largest gathering can be seen in Chepstow, when the Monmouthshire town teams up with their neighbours across the border in Gloucestershire for a celebration of Welsh culture and English morris dancing at the Chepstow Wassail and Mari Lwyd event.

The Mari Lwyd on the streets of Swansea during the Troublemakers' Festival. (Mark Rees)

The Land of King Arthur

At the end of the nineteenth century, Wirt Sikes wrote that 'in every part of Wales one encounters the ancient memorials of King Arthur', and that each of these places has its own 'legend, or its bundle of legends, poetic, patriotic, or superstitious'. This remains very much the case today, with landmarks steeped in Arthurian mythology to be found across the country. From the birthplace of his aid and magician Merlin to the scenes of some of his greatest battles, many of these places are easily accessible to the public and are best enjoyed after reading all about their connections with the King of Britons.

The Knights of the Round Table

When King Arthur wished to hold court with his gallant knights, he gathered the likes of Sir Gawain, Sir Lancelot and Sir Tristan around his legendary Round Table. It was diplomatically oval in design to ensure that everyone was seated equally, and its origins can be traced back to 1155 when it was first referred to by the Norman poet Wace in his translation of Geoffrey of Monmouth's *Historia regum Britanniae* (History of the Kings of Britain), the earliest book to detail the life of King Arthur.

While Geoffrey himself made no specific mention of a Round Table, he did popularise the idea of Arthur as a ruler who held court with his men, and placed a great deal of importance on one court in particular, the court of Caerleon inside

The bridge leading into Caerleon on a bright November morning. (Courtesy of Thomas Edwards under Creative Commons BY 2.0)

a 'walled city' in Wales. Just outside of Newport, Caerleon – which is more of a walled town than a walled city – was described as 'a delightful spot', and is where Arthur was crowned as king with a lavish feast following a hard-fought victory abroad. Its location 'on the River Usk, not far from the Severn Sea' made it the ideal venue for the many guests who would be arriving by boat, was very solid defensively, and was so aesthetically pleasing that aspects of it were even compared to the venerated capital of Italy, being 'remarkable for royal palaces, so that it imitated Rome in the golden roofs of its buildings'.

Maybe this comparison shouldn't come as too much of a surprise, as Caerleon has a long-standing connection with Rome which predates even the birth of King Arthur. For 200 years it played host to a Roman legion, and among the remains of the Roman legionary fortress Isca Augusta is a well-preserved amphitheatre where those stationed in Wales could spend their leisure time watching gladiators do battle. With eight entrances and a capacity to hold up to 6,000 people it was also used for parades and social events, and after being rebuilt on three occasions was abandoned in the fourth century.

It is this amphitheatre, which is now in the care of Cadw, that is said to be the location of King Arthur's Round Table. It has also been suggested that Caerleon could be the site of the fabled court of Camelot itself, although this is a claim which has several other contenders throughout Europe, including the

Caerleon amphitheatre. (Courtesy of littlemisspurps under Creative Commons BY 2.0)

nearby village of Caerwent. There are also many other places with a claim to being the home of the Round Table, such as two flat-topped hills in Wales which are both known as Bwrdd Arthur (Arthur's Table) in Llansannan, Conwy, and Llanfihangel Din Sylwy, Anglesey.

It is Caerleon, however, which has come to be accepted by many as Arthur's chosen court, and has attracted visitors for this very reason for centuries. When the English poet Thomas Churchyard wrote his description of Wales *the Worthiness of Wales* (1587), he emphatically noted in verse that,

> King Arthur sure was crowned there,
> It was his royal seat,
> And in this town did sceptre bear,
> With pomp and honour great.
>
> In Arthur's time a table round
> Was there whereat he sate,
> As yet a plot of goodly ground
> Sets forth that rare estate.

Caerleon amphitheatre. (Courtesy of Alun Salt under Creative Commons BY-SA 2.0)

A statue of King Arthur and Mordred's final battle at Ffwrwm Art & Crafts Centre, Caerleon. (Courtesy of Lee Russell under Creative Commons BY 2.0)

Merlin's Fort

Take a walk through Carmarthen's town centre and you could come face to face with arguably the most famous wizard in the world. Standing tall in the appropriately named Merlin's Walk is a life-size wooden sculpture of the Arthurian wizard which, like the man himself, has a magical origin story to tell.

The Welsh name for Carmarthen is Caerfyrddin, which translates as Merlin's Fort. Some say it is so-called because the magician was born there, while others believe that it is the other way around and that the character was named after the town. Either way, Merlin began life as the bard Myrddin Wyllt (Merlin the Wild) who, so the story goes, was driven to madness following the death of his master Gwenddoleu ap Ceidio at the Battle of Arfderydd in 573. He retreated into the woodlands to live as a hermit among the animals, during which time he gained the ability of prophecy, and thanks to these new powers the legend was born.

It was Geoffrey of Monmouth who began to popularise the idea of Merlin as we know him today by putting his own spin on Myrddin's mythology in his twelfth-century *Historia regum Britanniae*. He quickly became a staple of Arthurian adventures and, not only was it written that he was born in

The wooden sculpture of Merlin in Merlin's Walk, Carmarthen. (Courtesy of Llywelyn2000 under Creative Commons BY-SA 3.0)

Carmarthen, but he would later be killed there as well, by none other than his deceitful lover the Lady of the Lake.

Having wooed Merlin with the sole intention of stealing his knowledge, she turned it against him by magically shackling him in unbreakable chains and abandoning him to rot. Where exactly this took place is open to debate, but one contender is Bryn Myrddin (Merlin's Hill) in the village of Nantgaredig to the

Carmarthen Castle. (Courtesy of Tom Bastin under Creative Commons BY 2.0)

The new tree which stands near the site of the original Merlin's Oak in Carmarthen. (Courtesy of Regregex under Creative Commons BY-SA 3.0)

east of Carmarthen, his former home and an Iron Age hill fort thought to date from around 400 BC. In 1909, Marie Trevelyan wrote that he 'could be heard at certain seasons of the year bewailing his folly in allowing a woman to learn his secret spell' in his 'bonds of enchantment'.

Another popular piece of Carmarthenshire lore suggests that she might have cursed him at the site of another Merlin-related landmark, the so-called Merlin's Oak which stood on the corner of Priory Street and Old Oak Lane. The tree is said to have grown from his grave with his spirit trapped inside, and a dire prophesy attached to the oak predicted disaster for the town if it were ever to fall: 'When Merlin's Oak shall tumble down, then shall fall Carmarthen Town.'

That's exactly what happened in the nineteenth century when a tradesman threw caution to the wind and poisoned the tree to stop people from congregating under its branches. In order to avert disaster the remains were protected by iron railings until 1978, when the tree was removed to allow for the road to be widened. Yet ever mindful of the hex upon it, remains of the tree can now be seen in the foyer of St Peter's Civic Hall in Nott Square, which ensures that at least a part of the tree remains in the town centre, while another piece can be seen in nearby Carmarthenshire County Museum in Abergwili. A replacement tree has since been planted near the site of the original.

In a strange twist of fate, when Carmarthen's Greyfriars shopping centre was rebranded as Merlin's Walk in 2009, a wooden sculpture of the wizard was unveiled as its centrepiece. It was sculpted by woodcarver Simon Hedger who, years previously, had read in the local newspaper the *Carmarthen Journal* that a 500-year-old oak would be cut down to make way for the shopping centre, and claimed it for himself. He had no specific use for it at the time and so it sat in his studio for five years waiting for the ideal project, which arrived when he was commissioned to sculpt the carving of Merlin. All of which means that the statue we see today is made from oak which originally stood where the *Black Book of Carmarthen* (Llyfr Du Caerfyrddin), a thirteenth-century Welsh-language manuscript believed to contain the first reference to Merlin, was written by the monks known as the Greyfriars all those years ago. A magical coincidence worthy of the wizard himself.

Llamrei, the Trusty Steed

When King Arthur rode into battle, his steed of choice was his ever-dependable mare Llamrei, whose bravery more than matched that of the legendary hero she carried on her back.

Llamrei, as well as a stallion named Hengroen, first trotted onto the scene in the medieval Welsh prose tale Culhwch and Olwen. Lady Charlotte Guest wrote that the horse was 'very celebrated' in her nineteenth-century translation of the Mabinogion, and that her name implied 'bounding or curvetting'. Much like her rider she also left her mark on the Welsh landscape, quite literally in some cases, with two hoof marks created during their adventures serving as permanent reminders of her heroics.

The first print forms part of a monument on a footpath leading to Loggerheads Country Park near Mold. The memorial is a stone boundary marker which stands on the border of Flintshire and Denbighshire, and was erected in 1763 to resolve a heated land dispute. A plaque on the monument reads, 'The stone underneath this Arch CARREG CARN MARCH ARTHUR was Adjudged to be the Boundary of the Parish and Lordship of Mold in the county of Flint and of Llanverres in the County of Denbigh by the High Court of Exchequer at Westminster 10th November 1763.'

According to legend, Carreg Carn March Arthur, which means the Stone of Arthur's Horse's Hoof, was created when King Arthur was fighting with the invading Saxons on nearby Moel Famau, the highest hill in the Clwydian Range. With the enemy in hot pursuit his faithful horse leapt to safety and landed on the spot where the print can be seen today.

A second hoof mark can be found in Snowdonia National Park along a walking path leading to Llyn Barfog in Gwynedd. A marker stone there reads Carn March Arthur, and adjacent to it is the unmistakable curved mark in a stone in the ground.

Moel Famau from Rhosesmor. (Courtesy of ARG_Flickr under Creative Commons BY 2.0)

Carreg Carn March Arthur on the A494 road, marking the boundary between the lordships of Mold, Flintshire and Llanferres, Denbighshire. (Courtesy of Repton1x under Creative Commons BY-SA 3.0)

Above: Llyn Barfog. (Courtesy of Herne Hernesson under Creative Commons BY 2.0)

Below: Carn March Arthur near Llyn Barfog. (Courtesy of Herne Hernesson under Creative Commons BY 2.0)

According to legend Llyn Barfog, a small lake which means Bearded Lake, was home to an afanc, a terrifying lake monster from Welsh mythology. Its appearance varies wildly from tale to tale, ranging from a demonic entity to an oversized beaver crossed with a crocodile, but whatever form it took, it was large, dangerous, and not something to be messed with.

When the people of Aberdyfi turned to Arthur for help in ridding themselves of the monster he promised to do just that, and set off towards the lake astride Llamrei. He came prepared with a magical lasso and, after patiently waiting for the creature to surface, hooked its neck and urged the horse to drag it ashore. This was no mean feat and put great strain on the animal's legs, and as a result it left a hoof print in the stone below. Yet it persevered in its task and succeeded in pulling the afanc from its watery hiding place, and once on land they fought a fierce battle which Arthur would eventually win.

There are various endings to this tale and, depending on which one you chose to believe, the king either put an end to the creature's life then and there or, more humanely, relocated it to another lake far away from human activity. Either way, the people of Aberdyfi were safe once more and eternally grateful to be rid of the beast which had terrorised them for so long.

The Giant of Snowdon

Of all the Welsh landmarks with a connection to King Arthur, none has quite captured the romantic imagination like the majestic snow-capped peaks of Wales's highest mountain.

Known as Snowdon in English, which is thought to mean 'snow hill' in Old English, its Welsh name is the far more evocative *Yr Wyddfa* which, so folklore tells us, is named after the country's original BFG – a big ferocious giant. The giant in question was Rhitta (or Rhudda) Gawr, with gawr being the Welsh for giant, who ruled as the King of Wales from his lofty perch in the Snowdonian mountains. He was said to be twice as tall as the tallest man in the world, and was famed for being the meanest member of a race of super-sized beings famed for their meanness.

Britain was divided among thirty warring monarchs at the time, each of whom would have loved dearly to claim the lands of their rivals. Rhitta's land in particular was much sought after, but the giant himself had no desire in increasing his empire, and instead preferred to live a peaceful life away from all the squabbling. So weary was he of the other rulers' petty disputes and endless bickering that when he heard two kings named Nynio and Peibio quarrelling about which of them ruled the stars in the sky, he decided enough was enough and punished them in the most humiliating way possible – by cutting off their beards and hanging them from his belt.

A man's facial hair was considered to be a true symbol of his manliness at the time, and this act was seen as a great affront by all of the other kings. They decided to take revenge on Rhitta by uniting their armies and attacking as one,

Snowdon. (Courtesy of Daniel Damaschin under Creative Commons BY 2.0)

The summit of Snowdon. (Courtesy of Nathan Jones under Creative Commons BY-SA 2.0)

but even their combined might was no match for the warrior who not only defeated them but, to add insult to injury, claimed all of their beards and added them to his collection. When the rulers of other countries heard the reports of Britain's kings being left beardless they launched attacks of their own in a show of solidarity, only to suffer the same fate at the hands of Rhitta who amassed so many beards that he fashioned them into a cloak.

Yet there was one beard he did not own, the most coveted beard of them all: the beard of King Arthur. He sent a messenger to Arthur's court to inform him that, if he were to send him his beard, it would avoid any unnecessary bloodshed and would be given pride of place in his collection. Arthur, who had remained impartial until now, was furious with the request and sent the messenger back declaring that 'this is the most arrogant and villainous message that ever man sent to a king. By the faith of my body, Rhitta shall lose his head.'

He gathered his host and marched to Gwynedd, and when he found the giant their fight was brutal and relentless. Both sides landed blows strong enough to break the others' armour, their arms grew weary as the hours passed by, and blood and sweat clouded their vision. They were so equally matched that even as they weakened they remained in permanent deadlock, yet so offended was Arthur that, in a fit of extreme rage, he put every last drop of strength into one

Above: Llyn Llydaw. (Courtesy of Chen Zhao under Creative Commons BY 2.0)

Below: Y Lliwedd. (Courtesy of Nathan Jones under Creative Commons BY-SA 2.0)

final strike and brought his sword down hard on the giant's head. It landed with such violence that it broke through the helmet, through the flesh, and through the skull, cleaving Rhitta's head in two.

The giant was dead, and was buried where he fell at the summit of the mountain. Each of Arthur's men placed a stone on his final resting place, and the spot became known as Gwyddfa Rhitta, which means Rhitta's tumulus or burial mound. Over the years it became shortened to simply *Yr Wyddfa*.

Arthur's Stone

There was something troubling King Arthur ahead of the Battle of Camlann. As he walked along the golden sands of Carmarthenshire to meditate on the fight ahead, a fight which would prove to be his final showdown, an irritant far more immediate was disturbing his thoughts: a small stone trapped in his shoe.

The king removed the offending object and hurled it with so much anger that it flew across the Loughor Estuary to Gower where it eventually landed in Cefn Bryn, a 5-mile-long ridge in Reynoldston. Upon hitting the ground it swelled in size having been touched by the King of Britons, where it remains to this day as one of the area's best-known landmarks.

In reality, Arthur's Stone (Maen Ceti) is a giant capstone which forms part of a double-chambered Neolithic tomb in the centre of a round cairn. It is perched upon a group of smaller stones which, legend tells us, hold it aloft in veneration of it being the special stone which was handled by Arthur. Even for a capstone it is considered to be uncommonly large, measuring 4 metres

Arthur's Stone (Maen Ceti) on Cefn Bryn, Gower. (Mark Rees)

by 2 metres with a depth of 2 metres, but it was originally even larger still. A big chunk of stone which was once attached to the capstone can be seen on the ground next to Arthur's Stone which, according to Iolo Morganwg, was hacked off by Wales's patron saint St David in order to stop the druids from worshipping false gods. Other theories suggest that it was struck by lightning, or that a miller attempted to carve off a piece to use as a millstone but it proved to be too heavy to carry. Possibly the most likely theory is that it's exposed position on the hill simply led to it being naturally eroded by the elements, and a hairline crack caused it to fall.

Folklore tells us that the stone was once used by the 'young maidens' of Swansea to test the faithfulness of their sweethearts. They did this by visiting the remote spot at midnight during a full moon and placing a cake 'made of barley-meal and honey wetted with milk and well kneaded' upon it as an offering. They then crawled around the stone three times on their hands and knees and, if their lovers were true, they would appear before them. If they did not appear, this suggested that they were fickle in nature and best avoided. The stone was also said to be able to move of its own accord and, before dawn, would make its way to the nearby water for a drink.

Arthur's Stone was granted legal protection in 1882 under the Ancient Monuments Protection Act, one of only three Welsh monuments to receive such safeguarding alongside Pentre Ifan in Pembrokeshire, Wales's largest Neolithic dolmen, and Plas Newydd burial chamber in Anglesey.

The capstone of Arthur's Stone. (Mark Rees)

Inside Arthur's Stone. (Mark Rees)

Wild horses grazing opposite Arthur's Stone. (Mark Rees)

Mysteries of the Deep

Wales has long had a deep connection with the water. From the crashing waves of the sea to the rivers which criss-cross the land, it has been a bountiful source of food and work for the many people who live alongside it, yet a source of fear at times with its threat of the unknown always looming on the horizon. This dual nature of giving with one hand and taking with the other can be felt in some of the country's oldest stories, where tales of magical islands and beautiful water maidens are tempered with those of unfortunate souls who sleep in a watery grave.

The Mermaid of St Dogmaels

The mermaids of Wales share many similarities with their fish-tailed counterparts from around the world, with Welsh folklorist Revd Elias Owen writing in 1887 that they are 'above the waist a most lovely young woman, whilst below like a fish with fins and spreading tail'.

The mermaid sculpture at St Dogmaels. (Courtesy of Aberdare Blog under Creative Commons BY-SA 2.0)

They are fond of passing the time by combing their long hair by the water, and are generally very friendly when encountered, even falling in love with humans occasionally and inviting them to their homes under the sea. Yet Owen also urges caution when dealing with these unpredictable creatures, for their 'siren-like song was thought to be so seductive as to entice men to destruction'.

They have also been known to save the lives of those in peril on the high seas, as was the case of a young fisherman named Peregrine who lived in the coastal village of St Dogmaels. It was in 1789 that, as he sailed towards the headland of Cemaes Head, he spotted something moving on the rocks. He stopped his boat and crept closer for a better look, and couldn't believe his eyes when he beheld what appeared to be a beautiful woman combing her hair among the crashing waves. It was only as he got to within touching distance that he noticed the most remarkable thing of all: she had the tail of a fish in place of legs!

It was a real-life mermaid, and it was there in front of his very eyes. He determined to capture her in his fishing net, and so engrossed was she in grooming her blonde locks that she failed to notice until it was too late. On-board his ship his prisoner wept uncontrollably and, as much as he would have loved to have returned home with such a prize catch, it broke his heart to see another living creature so desperately sad. She pleaded with him to be released, and promised him a great reward in return, and with that he reluctantly returned

Cemaes Head. (Courtesy of Tom Bastin under Creative Commons BY 2.0)

Teifi Estuary from Poppit Sands. (Courtesy of brynivor under Creative Commons BY 2.0)

her to the sea. Before disappearing beneath the waves she thanked him for his kindness and promised to watch over him whenever he worked on the waves, and would warn him by calling his name three times in his hour of danger.

Time went by, and the mermaid soon became little more than an anecdote with which to try and impress his disbelieving friends and family. Yet while she might have been out of sight she still remained true to her word, and one fine day Peregrine heard his name being called three times from below his boat. 'Peregrine!', she cried. 'Peregrine! Peregrine!'

He could hear the voice as clear as day, and yet he assumed there must be some mistake. The sun was shining and there wasn't a single cloud in the sky, how could he possibly be in danger? Yet still his guardian angel implored him to pull in his nets and return to safety, and barely had he stepped foot back on solid ground when the sky blackened and an almighty storm erupted. It mercilessly whipped up the ocean waves and many a life was lost that day, but the mermaid had been true to her word and Peregrine survived unscathed.

Visitors to St Dogmaels will find that a wooden likeness of that heroic mermaid continues to watch over the waters today. Sculpted by artist John Clark from red cedar wood, it was unveiled in 2004 to mark the reunification of the former fishing village which had been split over two counties. It now sits entirely in Pembrokeshire but, before the redrawing of the boundary maps, had also been a part of Cardiganshire.

The Magic of May Day

In days gone by, a strange event would take place every May Day in the shadow of Pen y Fan mountain, south Wales's highest peak. At the stroke of midnight, an unassuming rock next to Llyn Cwm Llwch, a small mysterious lake with cool dark waters, would slowly creak open to reveal a secret passageway leading deep inside.

At the time, this remote spot in the Brecon Beacons had a reputation for being a bit peculiar, and was given a wide berth by all living creatures except for ravens. Yet if anyone did happen to find themselves in the vicinity on 1 May and venture into that curious opening, they would be in for a very pleasant surprise indeed, for that magical doorway led to an invisible island in the centre of the lake inhabited by scores of friendly fairy folk.

Those lucky enough to spend a day in their company would be entertained with joyous music, given their fill of tasty fruit to eat and, if they so desired, told predictions of what the future held in store. There was just one condition attached to these many tokens of their hospitality, and that was that nothing, no matter how small and seemingly inconsequential, was to be removed from the sacred island.

This rule was observed for many years until one visitor spoiled it for everyone by sneakily placing a flower in his pocket. All seemed well to begin with but, when the revels ended and he returned to mortal soil, he immediately paid a heavy price for his crime by losing his mind and spending the rest of his days as a mad man.

From that day forth the entrance never opened again, but the story lived on in local folklore and centuries later the people living nearby decided to drain the

Looking up Pen y Fan. (Courtesy of Ben Allen under Creative Commons BY-ND 2.0)

water to see if there was any truth to the old fairy tale and, more importantly, if any treasure had been left behind. They began by digging a trench, traces of which can still be seen today, and after a few short hours of hard graft they were within striking distance of breaking the bank. Just one more blow would release the water and reveal the secrets at the bottom of the lake and, as one man raised his pickaxe over his head to do just that, he was stopped in his tracks by a bolt of lightning which suddenly flashed through the air.

As if from nowhere a roaring thunder shook the earth beneath their feet, and the bright daytime sky turned as black as night. The men fled from the unnatural weather, and those brave enough to turn their heads back as they ran saw a ripple on the surface of the water shaking with increasing violence until a gigantic figure burst forth from the depths. It was that of a solemn-looking man with long hair and an even longer beard, and his furrowed brow suggested that he was far from amused. With the men now frozen in fright, he opened his mouth to deliver this ominous warning:

> If you disturb my peace,
> Be warned that I will drown
> The valley of the Usk,
> Beginning with Brecon town.

Llyn Cwm Llwch. (Courtesy of Claire Cox under Creative Commons BY-ND 2.0)

They did not need to be told twice, and from that day forth disturbed his peace no more. Yet they couldn't help but wonder how this giant of a man, as terrifying as he was, could submerge an entire valley with the water from such a small lake as he had threatened.

Above: The water flows through Pen y Fan. (Courtesy of sitye3 under Creative Commons BY 2.0)

Below: The Crannog on Llangorse Lake. (Courtesy of Phil Dolby under Creative Commons BY 2.0)

One of the older men of the party, Thomas Siôn Rhydderch, believed that he had an explanation. In his younger days he had thrown something into the lake, only for it to resurface days later while he sailed on a boat on the much larger Llangorse Lake. This was highly unusual because the two lakes were miles apart and were not in any way joined, yet there was no mistaking what he had seen. He concluded that they must somehow be magically connected with each other, and that if the smaller lake was in trouble then the larger one would come to its aid by 'discharging its vast body of water' on the surrounding land. Or to put it another way, if you mess with the little lake, its big brother will come and get you.

The Island of Love

Santes Dwynwen is Wales's patron saint of love, and her feast day, Dydd Santes Dwynwen (St Dwynwen's Day), is celebrated annually on 25 January.

In much the same way as St Valentine's Day, which commemorates the Roman saint of love on 14 February, it is a time for lovers to share tokens of their affections, with Welsh love spoons being a popular choice of gift. For adventurous lonely hearts it is also a time for attempting a little divination and casting love spells in order to glean some supernatural secrets about future partners.

One particularity romantic way to spend Dydd Santes Dwynwen is by visiting Ynys Llanddwyn (Llanddwyn Island), a small tidal island off Anglesey named after the saint who settled and established a church there. Legend tells us that

Ynys Llanddwyn. (Courtesy of Hanno Rathmann under Creative Commons BY-SA 2.0)

Dwynwen was one of the many daughters of Brychan Brycheiniog, a fifth-century king who fathered dozens of children, and as a young woman caught the eye of a Welsh prince called Maelon Dafodrill. They fell head over heels in love with each other and wished to be married, but her strict father had other plans. He had already arranged for Dwynwen to be wed to another member of Welsh royalty in a union which would prove to be very beneficial for the king's personal ambitions, and he would not have his daughter putting his plans in jeopardy.

When she broke the news to Maelon he took it badly. Very badly. In a fit of rage he lashed out, physically attacking her in some versions of the tale, and verbally attacking her in others. Either way the result was the same, causing the heartbroken princess to flee from the scene and seek solace in the woods where she found a quiet spot in which to pray. Being a devout Christian, she was sure that God would hear her prayers and come to her aid.

After hours of pleading for a cure to the pain caused by love she fell asleep, and as she slumbered among the trees two angels descended from Heaven to administer her with a potion which would do just that. Not only would it heal her broken heart but, in her dreams, she saw Maelon drinking a similar potion which froze him into a block of ice as punishment for his evil deeds. When Dwynwen awoke to discover her prayers had really been answered, she vowed to devote every minute of her life to God's service by protecting all true lovers.

The remains of St Dwynwen's Church. (Courtesy of TuK Bassler under Creative Commons BY-SA 4.0)

Above: Dwynwen's cross on Ynys Llanddwyn. (Courtesy of Alistair Young under Creative Commons BY 2.0)

Left: The Celtic cross on Ynys Llanddwyn. (Courtesy of Kevin Walsh under Creative Commons BY 2.0)

There were just a few loose ends to tidy up first, and she asked the angels for three more wishes. Sensing that they would be selfless wishes they were granted, and that proved to be the case. Her first wish was that Maelon should be thawed from his icy prison and allowed the opportunity to turn over a new leaf. Her second wish was to have the power to unite those destined to be together, or to cure heart sickness in those destined to part. Finally, her third wish was that she should never be married herself, in order to dedicate herself to God alone. This she did by taking the nun's habit and establishing a place of worship on an island just across the water from the village of Niwbwrch (Newborough).

The island remained her home until her death around the year AD 460, and in the centuries which passed became a popular place of pilgrimage for the faithful. The remains of a sixteenth-century church built on the site of the original church can still be seen today, as can two of the island's more distinctive landmarks, a highly decorative Celtic cross and a much simpler plain cross which symbolises Dwynwen's purity.

Devil's Bridge

The Ceredigion village of Devil's Bridge (Pontarfynach) gained its name, so the story goes, after Satan himself paid a visit and built the hamlet's distinctive bridge over the Afon Mynach river.

Anyone looking at the landmark today will see not one but three distinctive bridges stacked one upon the other, with the oldest at the bottom and the newest at the top. The most recent bridge is made from iron and was added in 1901,

Devil's Bridge railway station. (Courtesy of Tom Bastin under Creative Commons BY 2.0)

the middle bridge is made from stone and dates from 1753, while the original, which is credited to the Evil One himself, dates from between 1075 to 1200.

The well-known tale, as published in *The Welsh Fairy Book* (1907) by W. Jenkyn Thomas, begins with Megan, a hard-working old woman from Llandunach, feeling very sorry for herself on the banks of the Afon Mynach river. The heavens had suddenly opened causing a great flood, and now water was crashing more than 300 feet down the dingle into a swirling cauldron which 'whirled, boiled and hissed as if troubled by some evil spirit'. As a result Megan's cow, which was of great importance to the cash-strapped widow, was stranded on the other side of the water where, oblivious to its owner's plight, it simply chomped away at the tasty green grass.

She racked her brain for a solution and, as she mumbled 'Oh, dear, oh, dear, what shall I do?' to herself – or so she thought – a voice unexpectedly replied. 'What is the matter, Megan?' She turned to find a man dressed in a monk's cowl, and assumed that he had approached unheard due to the deafening sound of the water crashing all around. Wherever he had appeared from she was grateful for any help and, after explaining her predicament, the stranger came up with the perfect solution. It just so happened that building bridges was one of his personal amusements and, if she wanted, he would happily throw one across the chasm in order for her to reach her cow.

Devil's Bridge. (Courtesy of Alex Liivet under Creative Commons BY 2.0)

Megan was more than happy with the idea but, being a poor old lady, had no money with which to pay him. Undeterred, he simply replied, 'Just let me have the first living thing that crosses the bridge after I have finished it, and I shall be content.' She readily agreed, and the mysterious man instructed her to return and wait in her cottage while he set to work. Megan did just that but, being a wily old woman, had picked up on a few peculiar traits about the stranger during their conversation. For starters, his legs appeared to bend backwards, as if his knees

Below left: Devil's Bridge. (Courtesy of Peta Chow under Creative Commons BY 2.0)

Below right: Devil's Bridge Falls. (Courtesy of David Merrett under Creative Commons BY 2.0)

were on back to front, and what's more, he even appeared to have what looked like hooves attached to the end of them.

Assuming that it was Old Nick that she was dealing with, and that he was trying to trick her into giving away her soul, she concocted a plan with which to thwart him if needed. When she returned she took a loaf of bread with her, from which she tore and dropped small pieces in order to lure her small black dog along with her. The completed bridge looked impressive, and when Megan asked how strong it was its creator insisted that it was very strong indeed. 'Will it hold this loaf of bread?' she asked, to which he simply laughed and told her to throw it on to see for herself. She did just that and, as she did so, the dog chased after it, thus making her pet the first living thing to cross the bridge. With that the furious monk revealed his true nature and, with only a canine soul for his troubles, and not that of a human as he craved, disappeared as quickly as he'd appeared, leaving the lingering smell of brimstone in his wake.

Dog owners will be relieved to know that the Devil's parting words were that he had no use for the animal's soul, which ensured a happy ending for Megan, the cow, and the dog as well.

The Lady of the Lake

At first glance, Llyn y Fan Fach (Lake of the Small Hill) might look like a picturesque, if unassuming, body of water. But this beauty spot, which can be found off the beaten track in the Carmarthenshire section of the Black Mountain range, has a legendary tale to tell. For this 20-metre-deep pool in the shadow of Picws Du mountain was the scene of one of Wales' most well-known, and ultimately most tragic, folk tales.

The story begins in a nearby farm where a hard-working widow lives with her only son Gwyn. The young man was in charge of caring for the cattle who sometimes roamed as far as the lake to eat the sweet grass on its banks, and it was on one such occasion that, as the cows munched away, he noticed a rather unusual sight. The most beautiful woman he had ever laid eyes upon was standing in the middle of the lake, and so engrossed was she in combing her hair while staring at her reflection in the water that she failed to notice the awe-struck farmer boy gawping on. He knew immediately that this was a case of love at first sight, and stood transfixed as she drew her golden comb through her golden locks.

Gwyn was holding his lunch of barley bread and cheese in his hands and, without even thinking about his actions, stretched out his arms and offered them as a gift to his new-found love. As he did so she became aware that she was no longer alone and glided over to inspect his offering. With a playful smirk on her face she said 'Oh thou of the crimped bread, it is not easy to catch me,' and as soon as the words had left her lips there was a splash of water and she had vanished from sight.

That evening he spoke with his mother of the encounter, and they tried to decipher the cryptic message. It was decided that she must have been referring to the hard-baked bread, and that the love-struck Gwyn should return the following day and try again with uncooked dough instead. He could barely sleep with excitement and, before the sun had even risen, he was back beside the lake with dough in hands.

Llyn y Fan Fach. (Courtesy of Angel Ganev under Creative Commons BY 2.0)

He waited patiently as the minutes turned to hours, and as the sun reached its peak in the sky he began to lose all hope of a second meeting until, as if from nowhere, she miraculously materialised once more in the water. He held out his hands in anticipation but, as she inspected the bread, his hopes were dashed once more. Equally unimpressed with the gift she muttered 'O thou of the moist bread, I will not have thee' and returned under the waves, but not before giving Gwyn the briefest of heart-melting smiles.

Yet his elation at the smile soon faded with the realisation that he had failed to catch his sweetheart for the second time in as many days, and he walked home despondent. After consulting with his mother they decided there was only one option left, and if this 'lady in the lake' did not want hard bread or soft bread, he would return for a third and final attempt with half-baked bread. Sleep was even harder to come by that night and, after tossing and turning for some time, he rose at an hour when no other person in the land was stirring and returned to the lake. As with the previous day he waited and waited for the sun to rise, but this time the weather was not so fair and his companion was even less punctual. As day turned to afternoon and afternoon turned to evening, the only ripples that disturbed the face of the lake were created by the rain which drenched the land and soaked Gwyn to the bone.

He was all but ready to accept defeat when he noticed what appeared to be cows – yes, they were definitely cows – walking on the surface of the lake. He couldn't believe his eyes, yet there they were and, as he strained to see through the rainfall, noticed that behind the cattle was the lady he had long waited for. She looked more radiant than ever, and he could barely contain his excitement as he dashed into the water with hands outstretched. She gratefully took the bread from him and allowed him to escort her to land and, as he brought her ashore, he noticed that one of her sandals had been laced very strangely indeed. It wasn't her sandals

Above: Picws Du (Black Mountain), which overlooks Llyn y Fan Fach. (Courtesy of Claire Cox under Creative Commons BY-ND 2.0)

Left: The water flows towards Llyn y Fan Fach from the mountain. (Courtesy of David Evans under Creative Commons BY 2.0)

that he was particularity interested in though, rather it was her hand, and having been tongue-tied up until this point regained the use of his voice and blurted out 'Lady, I love you more than all the world besides and want you to be my wife.'

At first she resisted but, after listening to his promises agreed on one condition: he must abide by the rules of *tri ergyd diachos* (three causeless blow), which state that if he were to strike her three times without cause she would leave him forever.

Gwyn insisted that there was more chance of him chopping off his own arm than to strike her once, never mind three times, but as he pleaded his case she darted for the water and was gone once more.

Gwyn was now at the end of his tether. After three long days of trying to please his love he had finally succeeded, only for her to disappear yet again. He had reached rock bottom, and resolved to end it all by hurling himself from the highest rock into the very water from which she tormented him, and as he readied himself on the edge of the cliff he heard the voice of a man call out from behind him. He turned to see a wise-looking old man who was flanked on either side by two beautiful young women, both of whom perfectly resembled his beloved. Did she have a twin sister?

Addressing Gwyn as 'mortal', the man asked if it was true that he wished to marry one of his daughters. This he confirmed, and the man said he would agree to the union if he could select the correct daughter from the pair. Both women looked perfect in Gwyn's eyes, which left him with a terrible conundrum. He was faced with a 50/50 chance of a lifetime of happiness or one of unbearable regret, and he was all but ready to refuse the challenge until he noticed one ever so subtle difference. One of the women nudged her leg forward and there, on her foot, he saw the strangely laced sandal. He clasped her hands in his and, with that, the man beamed a large smile and congratulated them. True to his word the pair were to be wed and, if he took good care of Nelferch, as he discovered was her name, they would never want for anything again. This great bounty of riches began instantly with a dowry of countless sheep, cattle, goats and pigs, all of which magically emerged from the water.

They soon tied the knot and settled in a farm called Esgair Llaethdy. As the years went by they were joined by three baby boys and, when the eldest boy was seven years old, the happy couple were invited to a wedding. As they walked there Nelferch grew tired, and Gwyn offered to dash back home to get her a riding saddle and gloves if she caught a horse on which to ride in the meantime. When he returned to find his wife had not moved he playfully tapped her on the hand with the gloves and instructed to go and find a horse. What he'd failed to realise, however, was that this simple act counted as a strike and, with a sigh, she informed him that he had landed the first causeless blow.

Many years later they were at the christening of a baby, a bittersweet gathering as the little one was seriously ill and not expected to live much longer. As Nelferch wept in the pews Gwyn tapped her shoulder to comfort her, without realising again that he had dealt her a second causeless blow. From that moment on he had to be extra careful in his actions, knowing that one slip-up would be more than he could bear.

The Apothecaries' Garden and Hall at the National Botanic Garden of Wales, where a bed was added to show some of the plants used by the legendary Physicians of Myddfai. (Courtesy of Elliott Brown under Creative Commons BY-SA 2.0)

Sometime after the christening the poor baby did indeed pass away, and they returned to the church for the funeral. Rather than sob as she had on the previous visit, Nelferch burst out in laughter and all eyes were upon her. Her husband was mortified at her behaviour and placed his hand on her shoulder, demanding to know why she acted so inappropriately. She replied that she was simply happy that the child was finally at peace and no longer in pain but, now that the third causeless blow had been cast, she would not be so happy herself and would have to leave him immediately.

She gathered the animals from the farm and headed for the water from which they had emerged. A furrow which can be seen in the lake today was made by the oxen as they returned with their ploughs in tow. Gwyn was overcome with grief and once again determined to end his life by hurling himself from a great height into the icy black water. This time, there was nobody to intervene as he plummeted to his death.

Their three young sons, who were left to fend for themselves with nothing but an empty farm to their names, wandered aimlessly throughout the land. Then one day their mother unexpectedly returned one final time to tell them that they had a special mission to achieve on this earth, which was to relieve the pain and suffering of mankind. Having endured more grief in their short lives than most people experienced in a lifetime, they were perfectly suited to the task, and she taught them the art of natural healing. They rose to the challenge and became the famous Physicians of Myddfai, the most celebrated physicians in Wales who were rewarded with titles, land and privileges. But that, as they say, is a story for another day.

Tales of the Tylwyth Teg

Of all the magical creatures to appear in the tales of Wales, possibly the most numerous, and certainly the most unpredictable, are the wonderfully mischievous fairy folk. Better known as *y Tylwyth Teg* in Welsh, which translates as the fair folk or fair family, they are often described as being human-like in appearance, are unnaturally beautiful, and occasionally sport wings. Decked out in the most colourful clothes and no taller than a cat, they can pop up in the most surprising of places, but the best time to catch a glimpse of them is said to be at night when they dance a happy jig by the light of the moon. With the power to bestow blessings and curses on people it has long been thought wise to speak favourably of them and to treat them with kindness, as we shall see in this book's remaining stories.

The Fairies of Dinas Rock

In the Victorian era, the Vale of Neath had a reputation for being a stronghold of the 'fairy tribe', and their favourite spot was Dinas Rock (Craig y Ddinas), a gigantic limestone cliff on which thousands of fairies would dance to the music of the harp.

Standing tall over the village of Pontneddfechan in an area known as Waterfall Country, which is not only famed for its glistening cascades but, as we read earlier

Dinas Rock. (Mark Rees)

The rocks on the cliff edge of Dinas Rock. (Mark Rees)

in this book, is home to the Welsh water horse, the striking rock face once housed an Iron Age hill fort on its summit. It also takes its place in Arthurian legend as the location of Arthur's Cave, one of several places in Wales where King Arthur and his men are thought to be slumbering before awakening once more in the country's darkest hour.

In *Tales and Sketches of Wales* (1879), Charles Wilkins noted that members of the older generation living in the area earnestly believed in the existence of

Pontneddfechan. (Courtesy of Richard Jones under Creative Commons BY-SA 2.0)

y Tylwyth Teg, and one such believer, who is described as a level-headed old man not prone to flights of fancy, recalled an extraordinary story concerning his grandmother Maggy who made their acquaintance on several occasions.

The first encounter happened when she was a little girl collecting water from a nearby spring. As she filled her pail she sang a happy song, and was joined by what sounded like a bee humming along. She strained her ears to hear it more clearly, and realised that it was not a bee but somebody else singing as if in the distance. The volume rose and fell, and the song changed from a sombre lament to a jolly ditty, and so engrossed was she in the tune that she jumped in surprise when a voice next to her asked 'there, dear, how do you like it?'

It sounded like the voice of a little bird and, turning to look, she saw the smallest of men sitting on the edge of her pail, his feet kicking about in the overflowing water. The strange man looked very old in the face but very young in the legs, and his friendly bright eyes meant that her initial fear soon subsided. She asked him to sing again, and he agreed in return for a kiss. Maggy threatened to scream if he attempted to take such a liberty and moved to cover her face with her apron but, as quick as a flash, he sprang into her lap and placed a small peck on her lips.

The outraged girl did her best to slap the offending fairy but, having taken his kiss, he nimbly avoided her swinging arms and, true to his word, sang another song for her. This one was even more beautiful than before, and she could feel herself being lulled to sleep when she was disturbed by a shrill voice calling from afar. It was her mother demanding to know why there was such a delay with the water and, with that, she picked up her pail and the fairy had gone.

From that day forth he returned to the same spring many times to sing for Maggy, and on one occasion she asked him where he lived. He agreed to show her in return

A field near Dinas Rock, possibly the 'haunted' field where the fairies once danced in the moonlight? (Mark Rees)

for another kiss and, once again, before she had time to object he was on her lap and stealing one. He was too small to hold her hand and instead grabbed her dress with which to lead the way, and pulled her in the direction of his home. Yet as friendly as they had become over time, she was still a little apprehensive about leaving the familiar spot with a strange man and pulled herself free to remain where she was.

Afterwards, she would only see the fairy on one more occasion. Having grown into a fine young woman, it was as she walked home through a 'haunted' field at midnight with her boyfriend Jenkins that they came across a circle of fairies dancing in the moonlight. They crowded around the couple and playfully teased them for a while before returning to their revelries. All except one solitary fairy, that is, who broke ranks to cheekily tug at Maggy's dress for the final time.

The Verry Volk of Pennard Castle

While the fairy folk of Wales were popularly known as *y Tylwyth Teg*, there were also regional variations of the name. On the golden coasts of Gower they were commonly referred to as the Verry Volk, and a description of these impish creatures was recorded by W. Y. Evans-Wentz in *The Fairy-Faith in Celtic Countries* (1929).

The fairies of the peninsula were said to be generally warm-hearted unless crossed and, while they did much good, were also capable of the odd bad deed now and then. Often decked out in scarlet or green, they were fond of music and dancing in the moonlight, and would occasionally leave gifts behind for lucky mortals. One old woman always knew when she'd been visited because money would be found on the property, but this all came to a halt when she broke the fairies' golden rule and told someone of her good fortune.

Pennard Castle. (Courtesy of Gareth Lovering Photography under Creative Commons BY-SA 2.0)

On another occasion Miss Sarah Jenkins, postmistress of Llanmadoc, recalled how a man named William encountered the Verry Volk on his way to Swansea Market. They convinced him to join them in their dancing and, while this delayed his arrival at market, it only helped his sales after they rewarded him for his fine footwork, saying 'Will dance well; the last going to market and the first that shall sell.' He was indeed the first to sell.

Elsewhere on Gower, Eynonsford Farm was the scene of a far less fortuitous and much grislier encounter with the Verry Volk, where a farmer's dreams became a waking nightmare. It was late one night when the tenant was rudely awakened by the sound of sweet music and the patter of dancing feet, and he went in search of the source of the commotion. Gazing into the cow shed he found it 'filled with a multitude of little beings, about one foot high, swarming all over his fat ox', and worse still, not only were they swarming over his fat ox, they were ready to slaughter it.

Frozen in horror, he could do nothing but watch on helplessly as they killed, dressed, and then ate the poor creature. Yet the most remarkable part was still to come. Having eaten their fill they gathered all of the bones together save for one small leg bone which was lost during their feeding frenzy, and stretched the hide back over the skeleton. With that the ox rose up and was as fat, healthy, and as perfectly alive as it had been beforehand. When the farmer allowed the ox out

The view of Three Cliffs Bay from Pennard Castle. (Courtesy of Thomas Guest under Creative Commons BY 2.0)

Looking out from Pennard Castle. (Courtesy of WASD42 under Creative Commons BY 2.0)

the next morning it had a slight lameness in the leg which was missing the small bone, and which served as a reminder that he couldn't simply dismiss the events as a bad dream.

Possibly the most well-known encounter with these regional sprites took place at Pennard Castle which, according to legend, was built in a single night by a sorcerer for a particularly nasty Norman lord. It was on the day of that lord's daughter's marriage, when the castle was full of gluttonous guests overindulging in anything and everything, that news reached his ears of strange lights in the nearby woods. He gathered together some of his trusty men and set off to investigate, where they found the Verry Volk in the throes of a merry dance amongst the trees. The fairies were celebrating because they, like those in the castle, were happy that the young princess was now married. The lord, however, mistook their festivities as an act of aggression and, fearful that they might be working with the native Welsh against him, ordered his men to attack. A massacre ensued and very few survived but, standing tall in the centre of the bloodied bodies with tears streaming down her face was the queen of the Verry Volk. She stared deep into the eyes of the murderer and placed a curse upon his head with a single word: 'coward!'

As the lord peered out from his castle the next day, the weather served as an ominous tiding for what was soon to come. There were ink black clouds gathered in the sky on high, the waves crashed against the rocks with increasing violence,

The ruins of Pennard Castle. (Courtesy of Simon Gibson under Creative Commons BY-ND 2.0)

and all throughout the village an eerie screaming noise was heard blowing on the breeze. Some said it was the sound of the Gwrach y Rhibyn, the Hag of the Mist, who called out the names of those about to die. As the wind and rain battered the fortress, it was joined by the sand which rose in anger and smothered all those who dwelt within. There was so much sand that a great mound which disappeared in Ireland that night is thought to have been relocated across the sea.

The Verry Volk had taken their revenge and the remains of the castle are bewitched to this day, with an ill fate said to befall anyone who spends the night among the sandy dunes.

The Unwelcome Visitors

Fairies are unpredictable creatures at the best of times, and maybe the only thing that can be said for certain about these mischievous beings is that nothing is certain when it comes to the behaviour of the fair folk.

There are several tales in which the people of Wales came to the assistance of poorly dressed fairies by gifting them clothing of their own, a good deed which, you would assume, would be rewarded in kind. That was very much the case in one such story from Cwm Dyli in Gwynedd where a shepherd awoke in his hut one summer's day to find a fairy bathing her child. She had no clothing for the baby who was shivering in the chilly morning air, and the kind-hearted herder handed her one of his shirts to wrap around the 'poor thing'. She did just that, and did not forgot his generosity, ensuring that a shiny silver coin appeared in one his clogs for many years to come.

Cwm Dyli power station and Nant Gwynant. (Courtesy of John Englart under Creative Commons BY-SA 2.0)

Some fairies, however, take offence at such selfless gestures, and look down their noses at charity from mere mortals. Such was the case when similar events unfolded in the home of Morgan and Modlen Rhys, a married couple who lived in a farmhouse called Pen Fathor near the caves of Ystradfellte, the small village in southern Powys. They were not short of a pound or two, and all was well for the family until their idyllic life came crashing down when the lady of the house accidentally upset a fairy with her kindness.

It all began when Modlen spotted a poorly dressed creature in her house and handed it a new gown in which to clothe itself. The offended fairy snatched the gift from her hands and tore it to shreds, and soon after the family experienced what might nowadays be classed as ghostly poltergeist activity. When they were

The centre of Ystradfellte. (Courtesy of Morgan Owen under Creative Commons BY-SA 4.0)

in the kitchen they could hear a huge commotion taking place in the cow shed, and when they were in the cow shed they could hear a huge commotion taking place in the kitchen. Whenever they sat down for dinner dust would be shaken onto their plates from the crevices above, their crockery would be smashed at night, their cows were milked until they were dry, and their horses were ridden to exhaustion.

The family were at the end of their tether and needed help. Morgan first turned to a wise woman from Penderyn who suggested that they pack up their belongings and pretend to leave the house, thus tricking the fairy folk into thinking they had beaten them. Having announced that they had found a new home in Ystrad Tywi the family loaded the wagons and set off on their journey, when they encountered an old neighbour who asked where they were moving to. In reply a shrill voice rang out from a churn on top of a wagon that 'we're going to live in Ystrad Tywi'; far from leaving the family in peace, the fairies had instead hitched a ride and were planning on joining them in their new abode.

Having foiled their plan once, the unwanted visitors became even more vindictive, and attempted to snatch the Rhys's young baby from its mother's arms. Morgan again sought help, and this time turned to a cunning man in Pentre Felin who devised a plan based around the upcoming harvest. There was a big field near the farmhouse called Cae Mawr which would require a lot of help to

Sgwd yr Eira waterfall near Ystradfellte. (Courtesy of Richard Jones under Creative Commons BY-SA 2.0)

mow, and Morgan was instructed to speak with his wife about it on returning home. In a voice loud enough to ensure that the fairies could hear, Modlen asked her husband 'How many of the neighbours will be coming to help us tomorrow?' His reply was 'Fifteen of us in all, and you must see that the food is substantial and sufficient for the hard job before us.'

Modlen assured him that all fifteen men would be fed to the best of their means, but the next morning prepared the most measly, inappropriate meal that would barely sustain a single man for a day's hard work. When the fairies saw the spread, which consisted of a small sparrow roasted like a fowl, a dash of salt in a nutshell, and a small piece of bread, they realised that the family were already suffering enough without the need for them to make things worse. They declared that 'We have lived long: we were born just after the earth was made, but never have we beheld a sight like this. Let us quickly depart from this place, for the means of our hosts are exhausted. Who before this was ever so poor as to serve up just one sparrow as the dinner of fifteen mowers?'

The plan had worked, and that, dear reader, is how you rid your home of troublesome fairies.

The Afon Mellte river going underground near Ystradfellte. (Courtesy of Claire Cox under Creative Commons BY-ND 2.0)

The Saint and the Fairy King

The Denbighshire town of Llangollen is named after St Collen, a heroic holy man who, among his many legendary achievements, once went toe to toe with the king of the fairies and not only survived to tell the tale, but came out victorious.

The seventh-century monk spent much of his life travelling foreign lands, spreading the word of God far and wide before returning to Britain to take up the role of Abbot of Glastonbury. It was while travelling by coracle that he arrived in Wales, and founded a church where he landed on the banks of the River Dee (Afon Dyfrdwy). A medieval church dedicated to the saint still stands by the waterside today.

His encounter with the Fairy King came about after the pious brother, who was becoming increasingly concerned by the wickedness that he saw all around him, decided to seek solace in the mountains. He made a home for himself in a cell concealed by a rock, and while deep in contemplation he heard two men talking outside his door of a character called Gwyn ap Nudd, the king of the fairies and ruler of Annwn, the Welsh Otherworld, where supernatural creatures dwell.

This served to confirm his belief that the world was indeed in need of salvation, and so enraged was he by their blasphemous chitchat that he emerged from his exile to scold them for praising any lord other than the true lord of Heaven. Unmoved by his outburst they only laughed and warned him that to speak ill of Gwyn ap Nudd would result in a stern reprimand.

Llangollen. (Courtesy of Mark Warren 1973 under Creative Commons BY-SA 4.0)

The proud Christian took no heed of their words and returned to his abode but, soon after, there came a knock at his door. A strange voice enquired if it was Collen who dwelt within and, when he replied in the affirmative, the visitor explained that he was a messenger for Gwyn ap Nudd who demanded to meet with him at noon on top of the hill. Collen ignored the request and the next afternoon the messenger returned with the same summons. This was again ignored, and when the messenger returned for a third time he ended with the thinly veiled threat that 'If thou dost not go, Collen, thou wilt be the worse for it.'

This sent a shiver down his spine and he decided it would probably be for the best to meet this so-called king of the fairies, but not before he had first prepared a flask of holy water for the showdown. He arrived at the assigned location at the assigned time, and was amazed to find standing there the fairest castle he had ever seen. Minstrels and bards filled the air with beautiful music, while muscular men and playful maidens gave the illusion of it being a paradise as they frolicked all around.

Collen was invited into the great hall where Gwyn ap Nudd was seated on a throne of gold. He was surrounded by the finest delicacies known to man, and the future saint was encouraged to eat and drink his fill. In fact, any form of entertainment his heart might desire would be made available to him. Yet he stood firm and refused all of these earthly delights.

With a wry smile the king commended him on sticking to his principles, yet mocked him for turning down all of life's pleasures. He asked if he had ever witnessed such a spread of food and drink, or heard such wonderful music? And

The River Dee (Afon Dyfrdwy) in full flow. (Courtesy of Hefin Owen under Creative Commons BY-SA 2.0)

St Collen's Parish Church, Llangollen. (Courtesy of Peter Olding under Creative Commons BY-SA 2.0)

Inside St Collen's Parish Church. (Courtesy of Llywelyn2000 under Creative Commons BY-SA 4.0)

with a more menacing tone, he gestured to his soldiers and asked 'didst thou ever see men of better equipment than those in red and blue?'

Collen agreed that the king had much to offer, and that while his fairy troops were impressive, he noted that 'the red on the one part signifies burning, and the blue on the other signifies coldness'. With that he pulled out the flask of holy water from under his robes and threw it over the heads of the king and his troops, who instantly vanished from his sight. He had resisted temptation, and banished the pretender to the throne back to the Otherworld where he belonged.

The Swansea Valley Fairies

From the highest mountains to the darkest caves, the fairies of Wales have the remarkable ability of magically appearing wherever they are least expected. How exactly they whizz around the country so quickly had long been a source of speculation, until one farm servant accidentally discovered their secret when he just happened to be in the right place at the right time – or Ystalyfera, to be more precise – to catch them in the act.

Dai was out hunting for rabbits one day and hid behind a distinctive-looking rock in Ynysgeinon to wait for his prey. As he crouched there perfectly still with net in hand, an unusual-looking small man approached the stone and whispered a strange word to it. With that, a doorway leading inside the rock flew open and the man hopped inside, with the door swinging shut behind him.

Dai might not have caught any rabbits that day, but he did catch the secret password and, when his curiosity got the better of him, he did exactly as the small man had done and whispered it to the rock. Once again it opened and Dai entered, but this time it did not swing shut behind him. He tried to push it but it was just too heavy, and he realised that it would require some magical intervention to budge.

Ystalyfera. (Courtesy of pikeman180 under Creative Commons BY-SA 2.0)

Y Gaer Fawr (The Large Fort) on Garn Goch. (Courtesy of Niki.L under Creative Commons BY-SA 4.0)

As he considered his next move a loud commotion emerged from the darkness within. Another small man was charging towards him and shouting at the top of his voice that the draught from the doorway was causing the candles to flicker. This newcomer muttered a second strange word which closed the door and, as it slammed shut, Dai found himself trapped inside the rock and surrounded on all sides by hundreds of similar-looking small people.

As he was soon to discover, these were the mysterious passageways of the Cwm Tawe (Swansea Valley) fairies and, fortunately for the young man, they were more playful than malicious and decided to have some fun at the expensive of their nosey captive. He played along and, as a reward for being such a good sport, was allowed to live with them in luxury for many years to come. During this time he learned all about their series of intricate underground passageways which they used to covertly transport themselves around the country in order to steal dairy products from unsuspecting farmers.

Along with the one he had entered in Ystalyfera, they also had magical openings in Y Garn Goch, a historical hill in Carmarthenshire which is home to two Iron Age hill forts; another in the caves of Ystradfellte near the village of Penderyn, which leads to their beloved Waterfall Country; and in Dan-yr-Ogof caves, which is now the model dinosaur-filled National Showcaves Centre for Wales, which gave them access to nearby places such as Craig-y-Nos Castle where they could quickly appear and help themselves to butter, cheese and milk.

He also discovered that the fairies had a huge stash of gold tucked away in their lair and, after seven years in their company, decided to help himself to a hatful of guineas and make a sharp exit. On arriving back at the farm he told his

Underground in Dan-yr-Ogof Caves. (Courtesy of Nilfanion under Creative Commons BY-SA 4.0)

master all about his incredible adventure and, once the old farmer had seen the loot, not only did he believe the story but he set off to find the cave and claim some of it for himself. By following Dai's instructions he found and entered the stone without too much trouble, and once inside he gathered enough money for several lifetimes. Yet this still wasn't enough for the greedy farmer, who paid the ultimate price after being caught red-handed by the fairies on his second visit.

He was never seen again – well, not in one piece, anyway – and when Dai found his remains scattered nearby he was so disturbed that he vowed never to speak of it again. He took the password to the grave with him and, for a long time afterwards, the stone had a fearful reputation as a place to be avoided.

The Welsh dragon at Dan-yr-Ogof Caves. (Mark Rees)

Bibliography

Davies, Jonathan Ceredig, *Folk-lore of West and Mid-Wales* (The Welsh Gazette offices, Aberystwyth, 1911)

Ferris, Paul, *Gower in History: Myth, People, Landscape* (Armanaleg Books, 2009)

Guest, Charlotte, *The Mabinogion* (J. M. Dent and Co., 1906)

Howells, W., *Cambrian Superstitions* (Llanerch Publishers, 1991)

Jones, Edmund, *The Appearance of Evil: Apparitions of Spirits in Wales* (University of Wales Press, 2003)

Jones, T. Gwynn, *Welsh Folklore and Folk-Custom* (D. S. Brewer, 1979)

Owen, Elias, *Welsh Folk-lore* (Woodall, Minshall and Co., 1896)

Owen, Trefor M., *Welsh Folk Customs* (Gomer, 1994)

Parry-Jones, D., *Welsh Legends and Fairy Lore* (B. T. Batsford Ltd, 1953)

Pennant, Thomas, *A Tour in Wales part 2* (H. D. Symonds, 1781)

Rees, Mark, *The A-Z of Curious Wales* (The History Press, 2019)

Rees, Mark, *Ghosts of Wales: Accounts from the Victorian Archives* (The History Press, 2017)

Rhys, John, *Celtic Folklore: Welsh and Manx* (Oxford at Clarendon Press, 1901)

Roberts, Peter, *The Cambrian Popular Antiquities of Wales* (Cyngor Sir Clwyd County Council, 1994)

Sikes, Wirt, *British Goblins* (EP Publishing Limited, 1973)

Thomas, W. Jenkyn, *The Welsh Fairy Book* (University of Wales Press, 1995)

Trevelyan, Marie, *Folk Lore and Folk Stories of Wales* (Elliot Stock, 1909)

Wilkins, Charles, *Tales and Sketches of Wales* (Daniel Owen and Company, 1879)

Acknowledgements

Thank you to everyone who has joined me on this journey in search of Wales's weird and wonderful tales. In particular, I would like to wish a huge *diolch* to my family for their continued support, and to all at Amberley Publishing for commissioning the book that you now hold in your hands.

The stories contained within these pages have been brought to life by some wonderful photographs, and my thanks go to all of the photographers who have been individually credited throughout. Finally, a collection of this nature would not have been possible without the help of a great number of people, and I would also like to thank: Emma Hardy, *The Bay* magazine, The Comix Shoppe, Cymru Paranormal, Fluellen Theatre Company, Folklore Thursday, Phil Hoyles, the Lotus Sisters, Jenny White and all at Media Wales, Owen Staton, Rod Lloyd, Liz Barry, Wyn Thomas, my footballing companions Jean and Lindsay, and you, dear reader, for picking up this tome, a wise decision for which I'm sure the *Tylwyth Teg* will reward you handsomely.

About the Author

For more than fifteen years, Mark Rees has published articles about the arts in some of Wales's best-selling newspapers and magazines. His roles have included arts editor and what's on editor for titles including the *South Wales Evening Post*, *Carmarthen Journal*, *Llanelli Star* and *Swansea Life*. He has written a number of books on Welsh culture, with those of a supernatural nature including *Ghosts of Wales: Accounts from the Victorian Archives* (2017), *The A-Z of Curious Wales* (2019) and *Paranormal Wales* (2020). In 2017 he launched the now annual 'Ghosts of Wales – Live!' event, and in 2018, *Phantoms*, a play based on his ghost stories, was adapted for the stage by Fluellen Theatre Company and premiered at Swansea Grand Theatre.

Mark Rees. (Photo by Adrian White)